Spells for Love

Spells for Love

Antonia Beattie

Lansdowne

Contents

Love Spells

The Magic of Spells

Love is a powerful force that profoundly affects our lives. It is no surprise that love spells have been cast since time immemorial. Love spells exist for virtually every aspect of a relationship, from spells to discover your true love to those to help you recover from severe heartache.

Many traditions have evolved over the years concerning love spells. The symbol of the heart, the color red, and the beauty of the rose – all have strong vibrations with the emotion of love. These powerful symbols are some of the many ingredients and tools we will use in this book to help you find the happiness and sanctity of love.

The spells in this book are not traditional – they have not been passed down from generation to generation, but have been tailored to modern sensibilities to draw on and spread goodwill. A number of infamous traditional love spells were

designed to coerce a person into falling in love with a specific person or to wreak vengeance on a person for being unfaithful. This book does not contain spells that seek revenge or are coercive. These kinds of spells are considered unethical and dangerous. They should be avoided at all costs, as they attract the negative aspects of the golden threefold rule, which states that anything you send out will return to you at triple the strength.

We wish that the spells in this book help you find contentment and happiness within your own heart and in the hearts of your loved ones.

Simple Spellcraft

Spells can be cast by anyone, young or old. They are a safe and effective way of focusing on achieving the things you want from life.

All spells really require is a mind that can focus, an imagination that can visualize a goal being realized, and a soul that believes in a power higher than itself. This power can be a higher being, your own internal resources or a source of energy circulating within the earth itself.

Three steps are necessary before you cast a love spell. First, clear your mind of any unhappiness or anxiety about your love or your ability to find love. Imagine that you can put all your problems and worries into the palm of your hand. Now, imagine encasing these worries in a clear, pink bubble. Open the lid of a specially chosen box and imagine placing your bubble of worries into the box. Close the lid and put a piece of rose quartz crystal on the top, so your troubles cannot escape and worry you again.

Next, cleanse your body of everyday worries by having either a bath or a shower. If you are pressed for time, washing your hands will be sufficient, as long as you visualize that you are washing all the thoughts of the day away from you.

The third step is to prepare your room or special space for the spell casting. If you feel particularly troubled, cast a blue circle around you as you settle down to do your spell – imagine a line of blue light traveling in endless patterns around you in a circle. Make sure that you have all your ingredients and tools with you before you cast your circle, to avoid having to break the line.

You are now ready to do some spellcraft.

Spell Tips

Follow the instructions for your chosen spell carefully. We will tell you the ingredients required, the tools you need and the best time to cast the spell. Love spells are usually cast on a Friday, the day that resonates with Venus, the Goddess of Love.

As you will see from most of the instructions, spells are not simply putting together a few ingredients on a particular day. They need to be fueled with thought and energy.

When preparing any spell, keep your mind focused on everything you are doing and every ingredient of the spell.

Take time to smell the herbs deeply, feel each bump and crevice of your stone, and appreciate the color of your candle.

During the preparation of the spell, choose a simple sentence that sums up what you are planning to do, and repeat it aloud while you are gathering the ingredients, sewing your spell bag or carving a word into a candle. For example, in the spell for finding your true love, repeat as a mantra during the whole time you are preparing the spell:

"I shall find my true love. I shall find my true love."

During the whole time you are preparing and casting your spell, make sure that you feel linked with the earth. Be conscious of your feet and feel the energy of the earth rising up, like a golden light, through your legs and trunk and out through the top of your head.

Visualize this energy flowing back down into the ground and rising up through your feet and body again. Once your spell is cast, focus again on this flow of energy to feel grounded and reconnected with your body.

Is Anyone Out There?

Attracting Love Into Your Life

What do I need?

A plain white sheet of paper

A pair of scissors

A red pen

A black pen

Two pink roses

A bowl of water

This spell is designed to help you attract love in all its forms into your life. The spell will allow you to feel that you are worthy of love. It will also give you the power to attract all sorts of love – the love of your parents, friends, workmates, in fact, everyone with whom you come into contact.

What should I do?

Take a sheet of plain white paper and cut the sheet in half. Using a red pen, write down on one of the two sheets all the things that you feel make you lovable.

Then, with a black pen, write on the other sheet of paper all the things you can think of that you feel make you unlovable.

Near a window, place the two roses in a glass jar on top of the positive sheet, which has been written in red ink. This will start the spell of attraction.

Place the negative sheet in a bowl of water and watch it disintegrate and the ink of the black pen run until it is no longer legible. Throw out the soggy sheet.

Keep the positive sheet and jar in place for 28 days – the full cycle of the moon. For example, if you start this spell on a full moon, it ends on a full moon. Change the flowers as soon as they start to droop.

When should I do this spell?

Any time you feel unloved and alone

Improving Your Self-esteem

What do I need?

Four drops of rose geranium essential oil

Two naturally-colored beeswax candles and two candle stands

A full-length mirror

Feeling happy and vibrant can itself attract love. If you feel less than vivacious, it could be because you have a low sense of self-esteem. Allow yourself a few treats and avoid running yourself down. Also try this grounding spell, which will help you feel connected with the nurturing power of mother nature.

What should I do?

Sprinkle two drops of rose geranium essential oil at the base of the wick of each candle. Light the two candles and place them on either side of the full-length mirror. Step back so that you can see a reflection of your face and torso.

Look at your feet. Imagine a line of golden light is entering your body through your feet. This light is coming from the ground and symbolizes the flow of the earth's energy.

Allow this golden light to travel through your body and up through your head. Visualize the light coming out of the top of your head like a fountain. As the light showers over you, imagine that it is encasing you with a nurturing energy.

Chant the following affirmation:

"I can be who I want to be."

Feel nurtured for who you are and who you can be. If you feel that too many negative voices are interfering with this spell, just shift your focus to the feeling of receiving energy from the ground, or to "seeing" a golden glow around you. Try this exercise for three evenings in a row.

When should I do this spell?

During a full moon

Attracting a New Friend

What do I need?

A blue non-drip candle

Two or more drops of cedarwood essential oil

A clean cloth to wipe your hands on

A knife with a point sharp enough to carve into the candle

A bowl half-filled with sand within which the candle can stand overnight

There are many popularity spells. The best spells are those asking for someone to appear who will be a good friend for you. Like a lighthouse, the spell below creates a beacon effect, signaling that you are open to finding new friends, and catching the subconscious attention of the people around you.

What should I do?

Take the candle and rub the two drops of cedarwood essential oil along its length. If you have chosen a tall or thick candle, you can use two more drops of oil.

When the candle is coated, wipe your hands on the cloth. Use the knife to carve the words "New Friend" or "New Friends" along the side of the candle.

Then place the candle in the bowl. Light the candle and stare into the flame, imagining having an outing with a good friend.

When you have finished your visualization, place the candle on a high ledge in your home near a window (preferably one without curtains).

Make sure it is safely upright and away from anything flammable. Leave the candle to burn itself out during the night.

When should I do this spell?

On a Thursday, preferably when the moon is waxing (growing fuller)

Attracting a New Lover

What do I need?

A round piece of red leather or silk, approximately 6 inches (15 cm) in diameter

Two drops of patchouli essential oil

A small rose quartz crystal (pink), preferably in the shape of a heart

A copper coin (or a round, flat piece of copper sheet)

Approximately 4 inches (10 cm) of thin, flexible copper wire

The following spell is designed to help attract the most suitable person to be your lover. Copper is an important ingredient in love spells, as it is believed to be the metal associated with the Goddess of Love, Venus.

What should I do?

Sprinkle the two drops of patchouli oil onto the piece of leather or silk. Place the small rose quartz crystal and the copper coin or disk onto the fabric and take up the ends of the cloth to form a small pouch.

Use the copper wire to tie the ends of the cloth together.

Hold the bag in the palm of your hand and allow your body warmth to heat the oil that has soaked into the fabric. You will soon be able to smell the scent of patchouli.

As you are holding the bag, visualize the type of lover you wish to attract. Be specific, and as graphic as you like. Imagine that the image of your new lover is being encoded into the copper coin or disk and the stone.

Carry this bag until the next phase of the new moon or when the lover you want appears in your life – whichever comes first.

When should I do this spell?

On a Friday, preferably during the phase of a new moon

Finding a Soul Mate

What do I need?

A tall, narrow candle, preferably white or silver

A pair of scissors

A sharp knife

About 12 inches (30 cm) of thin, flexible copper wire

A white cloth made from natural fibers

A soul mate can be either a very close friend or a lover (or both) – a person who gives you a feeling of being complete. A soul mate can be someone who shares your views, interests and outlook on life, or a person who complements your personality, making a partnership of opposites with mutual respect for each other's strengths.

What should I do?

You will need to do this spell over a three-day period. Break the candle into two pieces, and use your scissors to cut the wick between the pieces. Use the sharp knife to cut wax from the wick on the bottom half of the candle, so that both halves of the candle have an exposed wick that is long enough to light.

On the first day, place the candles apart in the furthest corners of your home. On the second day, place the candles a little bit closer to each other, but still apart.

On the third day, place the candles side by side in the middle (or heart) of your home. Tie them together with the copper wire, letting the wire spiral evenly around the candles, and light their wicks.

When the candles burn down to the first strand of copper wire, extinguish the flames and imagine that the smoke is rising up to search for your soul mate.

Keep the candles stored in a safe place, wrapped in the white cloth.

When should I do this spell?

On a Friday, when the moon is waxing (growing fuller)

Finding Your True Love

What do I need?

A sapphire (preferably unset) or a dark blue glass bead

Several handfuls of dirt or sand

A bowl

Spells to find your true love are very popular and take many forms. If you are seeking to find a true love who will contemplate matrimony, one of the best spell ingredients is a sapphire. The sapphire is symbolic of faithful and contented love. If you can't get a sapphire, substitute a glass bead of deep blue.

What should I do?

Wash the sapphire or glass bead under running water. Get a few handfuls of dirt or sand from your garden or from a garden supplies shop.

Place the dirt and your sapphire or blue glass bead in the bowl. Swish the dirt around so that you lose track of where exactly your gem or bead is within the bowl.

Take a moment to visualize yourself feeling happy and relaxed with a person you love deeply. With that thought in mind, sift your fingers through the dirt, trying to sense where the gem or bead is hiding.

When should I do this spell?

On a Friday, when the moon is waxing (growing fuller)

Use only the hand that you write with to search through the dirt, and use your intuition to help you locate the gem or bead. When you do find it, your spell is cast. Carry the gem or bead with you for a full cycle of the moon – 28 days.

The Dating Game

Feeling Attractive

What do I need?

A hand mirror with a handle

9 ½ inches (24 cm) of thin flexible copper wire

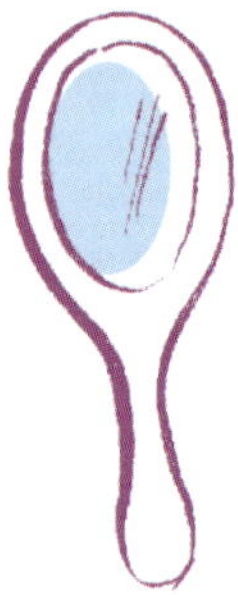

An important rule to remember as you are preparing for an important date is that you are as attractive as you feel. No matter how beautiful or handsome you actually are, if you are feeling lousy and unattractive, this will show through. So one of your first tasks is to start your preparations for that important date by focusing on the inside.

What should I do?

Stand outside or in a room where you feel safe, with your hand mirror face down at your feet and the copper wire in your hands. Face the direction of the nearest large body of water. This direction corresponds with the element of water, which in turn relates to our emotions.

Imagine the earth's energy coming up through your feet and the rest of your body into your hands, and allow the energy to mingle with the copper wire. Copper is an excellent conductor of psychic energy. The earth's energy will help stabilize your feelings and help you realize your potential.

When you feel ready, pick up your mirror and wrap the wire in spirals around the handle. Twist the ends so that the wire does not unravel. Look into the mirror and say the following words 33 times:

"Tonight I shall fulfill my potential and be an attractive person."

Once finished, move your feet to disconnect from the earth. Feel the energy still circulating around your body. Prop the hand mirror on your dressing table or chest of drawers so that it is reflecting a harmonious picture, such as the view outside your window or a bunch of flowers, and continue with the rest of your preparations for the date.

When should I do this spell?

Any time before a date

Looking Your Best

What do I need?

A dressing table mirror or full-length mirror that can be tilted so you can see your head and some space around it

A piece of glossy red, green, or purple paper

Auras are colors that indicate certain vibrations of energy around you. Some gifted people may see auras around a person's body or head. Judging by how far the color is flaring from the body and what colors are flaring in certain areas of the body, they can tell us what emotions we are feeling and what areas are experiencing energy blockages. You can work with your aura to help you feel prepared for your date.

What should I do?

The first step is to practice seeing your aura. Sit or stand in front of your mirror. If possible, have a dark or white background behind your head. Stare at the area around your head (the aura in this area is called a nimbus). When your eyes get tired of staring, half-close your eyes and see if you can sense any shadows or colors around your head.

Usually, if you are nervous, the shadows or colors in this area are very close to your head.

Now imagine one of the following colors flaring around your head. This is a way of invoking the corresponding feeling, not only within yourself, but also in the form of an energy that will be subconsciously picked up by your date:

- Purple – calm and controlled
- Red – sexy and attractive
- Green – earthy and stable

Once you feel that you have visualized the appropriate color around your head, cut out a square of paper that corresponds with the color you have chosen and fold it so that it will fit into your pocket, wallet or purse. Carry the colored paper with you during your date.

When should I do this spell?

Any time before a date

Increasing Your Feelings of Confidence

What do I need?

A mirror

A picture or symbol of your totem animal – choose an animal that embodies the attributes or confidence that you wish to carry with you into the date. Consider one of the "big cats," such as a panther, lion or tiger, or some of the lighter, more graceful creatures, such as a gazelle

A white or natural-colored candle and a candle stand

Sometimes we need an extra burst of energy to help improve our confidence. Being told that we are attractive or desirable is always helpful, but we can't rely on being told these things when we actually need to hear them (and without needing to prompt the person). Tapping into a confident energy that is constant is a desirable way of improving your sense of assurance. The following spell creates a totem animal that can accompany and protect you on the most nerve-wracking of dates.

What should I do?

Use an adhesive that is easy to remove to stick a picture of your chosen totem animal to the glass of a mirror, just above eye level. Sit in front of the mirror. Light a candle and place it in a candle stand so that it is stable and you won't be distracted if the wax drips. Place the candle in a position where you can see both the picture and the candle flame.

Concentrate on the flame. Within the flame, imagine seeing yourself as you meet your date. Are you feeling nervous or ill at ease?

If so, look up at the picture of your totem animal. Superimpose the poise and confidence of your totem animal over your image of yourself on the date.

Now lock that image of yourself feeling confident in your mind by taking the picture of the animal off the mirror and passing it over the flame. When you feel ready, blow out the candle. Carry the picture with you on your date.

When should I do this spell?

Any time before a date

Improving Your Communication Skills

What do I need?

A small table

A blue stone, such as a turquoise

A stick of cedarwood incense

A cup of cooled caffeinated tea

A green bowl full of mushrooms

A white candle and a candle stand

A box of matches

A handful of coffee beans

A number of important energy centers run through your body, close to your spine. Each energy center corresponds with a color, and with important aspects of your life. To improve your communication skills you need to activate your throat chakra, which is situated in the hollow at the base of your throat, just over your larynx.

What should I do?

Set up a small table in your room or somewhere outside where you will not be disturbed. Place your stone on the center of the table. Around the stone, place the incense, the cup of tea, the bowl of mushrooms and the candle. Light the incense and the candle. These four ingredients represent the elements of air, water, earth and fire. Scatter the coffee beans around the stone.

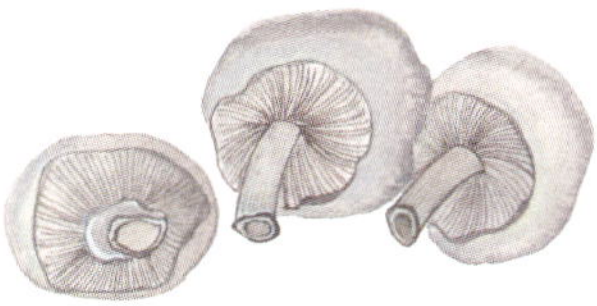

When you have finished these preparations, pick up the stone from the middle of the table and place it at the base of your throat. Feel the stone's power protecting you against criticism, allowing you to speak freely. Concentrate on this feeling, and allow yourself to talk. Say anything, even if it is just random syllables.

When you feel your speech is flowing well, take the stone away from your throat and pass it over the incense, tea, and mushrooms, then carefully pass the stone over the flame of your candle.

Carry this stone with you in your pocket or purse when you go out on your date.

When should I do this spell?

Any time before a date

Staying True to Yourself

Never be tempted to be something or someone that you are not. Staying true to yourself is one of the most fundamental tools in achieving a lasting, loving relationship. Being loved for who we are is much more satisfying than molding ourselves to what someone else wants us to be. Try to resist this type of manipulation by casting the following spell. It will help you to gain a true sense of who you are and to keep that knowledge during your date.

What do I need?

A lock of your hair

Some of your nail clippings

A passport-size picture of yourself smiling

A royal blue-colored cloth bag, big enough to contain the picture, the hair, the nail clippings, your list, and some unhulled sunflower seeds

What should I do?

Put the lock of your hair, your nail clippings and your photograph into the royal blue cloth bag. Sit comfortably in your favorite room, chair or space. Have the little bag sitting in your lap.

also ...

A favorite pen

A small piece of paper (about B5 size: 9 ⅞ x 6 ⅞ inches / 25 x 17.6 cm)

Eight sunflower seeds still in their shells

A length of a black leather thong or thin silk ribbon

With your favorite pen, write down on the sheet of paper the positive qualities that define who you are, such as good humor, optimism, liveliness or thoughtfulness. Also write down what you like and dislike generally, and what you like and dislike in a relationship.

Take time to put a really good list together. Fold the paper and place it into the blue bag. Pour in the sunflower seeds, then tie the bag with the leather thong or silk ribbon.

Carry the bag with you on the date to remind you of your worth, and of who you truly are.

When should I do this spell?

Any time before a date

Enhancing Your Love & Friendship Skills

Learning to Listen

Try this spell to renew your ability to listen to each other without negativity. This spell can be done with your loved one, or performed by yourself (simply imagine your loved one sitting with you).

What do I need?

Two blue comfy cushions or chairs covered with blue cloth

A small table

Two blue or purple candles and two candle stands

A stick of lavender incense

A plate of sweet cookies (home-baked, if possible)

Two cups or glasses of hot chocolate or good quality coffee

What should I do?

Position the cushions or chairs so they are opposite each other, there is enough space to walk around them, and no one has their back to the door. Put the small table between the chairs so that it is within easy reach. Place the candles, incense, drinks and plate of cookies on the table.

If you are doing this spell with someone else, allow him or her to sit in a chair or on the cushion while you walk around the chairs in a circle three times, ringing the bell to disperse negativity. Try to leave any arguments outside the circle.

Light the candles and incense before sitting down to drink and eat in silence together, becoming aware of the energy between you. If you are performing the spell alone, visualize the energy of your relationship surrounding you. Allow the sweetness of the tastes to flavor the energy flows, changing them from negative emotions to deeper, more loving ones.

When both of you are ready, blow out the candles and extinguish the incense. Imagine the circle around you dissipating. Wrap each candle in a piece of cloth and give one to your partner or friend. Light your candle whenever you want to be listened to.

also ...

A melodious-sounding hand bell

Two pieces of blue or purple cloth made from natural fibers

When should I do this spell?

Whenever you feel tension in a relationship or friendship. If you want to tap into a time when psychic channels are open, do this spell during a full moon.

Encouraging Faithfulness in Your Lover

What do I need?

Brown cloths large enough to cover the mirror or mirrors in your bedroom

A two- or three-dimensional representation of two ducks

Spells to make another person act against their will or be something that they are not are unethical and should not be attempted. However, there are two ways in which you can encourage faithfulness in your lover.

First, if you want to receive the gift of faithfulness from your lover, you will need to pay the compliment of being faithful yourself. Second, a very simple ethical spell exists that will encourage the energy to flow harmoniously between you and your partner.

Before doing the spell, count how many mirrors are in your bedroom. You will need a cloth to cover each mirror. According to feng shui beliefs, a mirror in the bedroom is bad luck for a relationship because it is symbolic of a third person in the bedroom.

What should I do?

Walk to each corner of the bedroom and clap your hands to disperse negative energy. Also clap your hands over the pillows on your bed. Open the windows of your bedroom and imagine the negative energy flowing out of the room.

Clap your hands in front of each mirror in the bedroom and then throw a cloth over the mirror. Place the representation of the two ducks in front of the main mirror in the room and leave them in place until your partner comes home.

Consider revamping your bedroom so that the mirrors can be covered when they are not being used.

When should I do this spell?

Whenever your partner is away from you. If you want to change an already present fear, cast this spell at new moon.

Encouraging Loyalty in Your Friends

What do I need?

One sheet of letter-size paper

A black pen

A pair of scissors

A small wooden box with a lid

A single pearl or a pearly opalescent bead

A pink ribbon

In magic, there is a belief that like attracts like. If you are a loyal person, you will tend to attract other loyal people. But if you are known to talk about people behind their backs, you may need to correct this tendency before doing this spell.

What should I do?

Take the sheet of paper and write the word "loyalty" in letters big enough to cover the entire page, imagining the people from whom you seek this kind of support. Turn over the page and write their names in full.

Take a pair of scissors and cut the sheet of paper into long thin strips. When you have finished, scrunch and roll the strips into a nest that will fit into your box.

Place the paper nest in the box and position the pearl or pearly opalescent bead on top of it. The pearl is symbolic of loyalty. Close the box and tie the pink ribbon around it.

When should I do this spell?

During the phase of a new moon or any time when you need the help of your friends

Hold the box in your hands as you visualize a comfortable cocoon of loyalty being woven around you by the spell. Place the box at a window that gets the morning sun or take it with you when you need support to face a crisis.

Reviving a Flagging Relationship

What do I need?

Something from the time of your honeymoon or your early days of courting (such as pressed flowers or a negligee)

A piece of red cloth made from natural fibers

A moonstone

A sprig of rosemary

Modern stresses and strains can take their toll on a relationship, no matter how devoted the couple is to each other. Try the following spell to rekindle your loving relationship. The spell features a moonstone, which can either be a loose stone or one mounted in silver. Moonstone contains vibrations that help revive a flagging relationship. If the moonstone is mounted in silver, this also attracts the psychic powers of the moon.

What should I do?

Choose something soft or small that represents the early days or happy times of your relationship. When you have found the right symbol, wrap it inside the red cloth with the moonstone and the sprig of rosemary.

Place the package under your pillow. As soon as you awake in the morning, jot down any images or sequences that came to you in your dreams. These dreams may give you an indication of what you may need to do to rekindle your relationship.

If your dreams do not give you enough information, continue to sleep with the package under your pillow for three nights. A solution will soon become obvious to you.

After three nights, unfold the package. Hang the sprig of rosemary over your bed until the next new moon to encourage the flow of positive energy into your relationship.

When should I do this spell?

During the phase of a new moon

Reviving a Sense of Goodwill and Respect

What do I need?

A silver bowl full of water

A rose quartz crystal ball

Generosity and goodwill are important factors for a happy, long-lasting relationship. If you are in a tense relationship, try changing the flow of energy in the relationship from negative to positive by focusing on finding and appreciating aspects of your partner's or friend's character that you respect.

Try to honor these character traits for three days and nights, and see if there is a shift in his or her behavior toward you. This is often all that is needed to change the dynamics of a relationship for the better. If you feel too angry to do this, try the following spell.

What should I do?

The silver bowl full of water in this spell is symbolic of the nurturing energy of the moon. Sit in a special place – either inside or outside – in view of the new moon, and gaze into the bowl of water. Visualize yourself bathing in the water, washing away all your anger and frustrations in the relationship.

When should I do this spell?

During the phase of a new moon

When you feel ready, pick up your ball of rose quartz crystal and cleanse it in the bowl. Enjoy the sensation of water gliding over the smooth, rounded stone. Visualize the potential of your relationship and recognize your commitment towards infusing it with generosity and goodwill.

Pour the water back into the earth. Keep the stone with you whenever you are communicating with your partner or friend.

Learning to Trust

What do I need?

Each of you choose a sample of your favorite foods, drinks, music, soft-textured materials, feathers and scents

A blindfold

This is a fun spell that you can do together with your partner. It is also a useful spell to help revive your relationship by attuning all your senses to each other.

What should I do?

Sit in a comfortable area, on the bed or on cushions on the floor, at a time when you will not be disturbed. Take the phone off the hook. Arrange all your favorite things around each of you.

Blindfold your partner. Play a piece of your favorite music, and while it is playing, present him or her with one or more of your perfumes or favored aromatherapy essential oils. Glide fabrics over his or her skin and feed him or her the choicest samples of your favorite foods, or let him or her sip your favorite drink.

Take the blindfold off and gaze into each other's eyes. Drink in the beauty of your love for each other. Allow your partner to blindfold you and show you his or her favorite things.

This is a lovely, bonding spell that can be improved with the exchange of kisses between each sensation shared.

When should I do this spell?

During the phase of a full moon

Spells to Show You Care

What do I need?

An oil burner filled with water

Four drops of lavender essential oil

Four drops of rose geranium essential oil

A tea light and some matches

A comfortable chair

A small amethyst

A purple bag made from natural fibers, large enough to contain the amethyst

Honoring Yourself: Creating a Circle of Love

This is a nurturing spell – it creates a loving energy field that wraps around you, both protecting and nourishing you. It is based on a guided meditation that encourages you to feel loved and cherished. This feeling is anchored into a stone that you can carry with you in times of loneliness, trouble, or deep unhappiness.

What should I do?

Prepare your oil burner by measuring the lavender and rose geranium essential oils into the bowl filled with water and lighting the tea light. Sit comfortably in your chair and hold the amethyst in your hand.

Concentrate on your breathing, breathing in for a count of four and out for a count of four. When you feel ready, imagine yourself standing in a beautiful glade covered with soft grass and dappled sunlight. A dense forest surrounds the glade.

Visualize, through the trees, a beloved family member or friend coming to join you in the glade. This person may be alive, or someone who has passed away. Embrace your relative or friend, then let him or her stand a little away from you.

Now imagine other people coming toward you – everyone you know who cares for you. Allow your conscious mind to invite those you may not know yet but who will be important to you in the future. Embrace each person and watch them all form a circle around you.

Visualize the energy emanating from this circle enfolding you in a pure light. Allow yourself to feel deeply joyful and warmly appreciated. Feel this energy concentrating into your amethyst.

When you are ready, say goodbye to your circle of loved ones and concentrate again on your breathing. Open your eyes and feel the glow of energy from your stone. Place it in the purple bag and extinguish the tea light in the oil burner. Keep this stone under your pillow to give you a restful night's sleep.

When should I do this spell?

Any time you are feeling down

Honoring Your Relationship: Preparing a Love Feast

What do I need?

A rose-colored candle

Your loved one's favorite foods

A bunch of red flowers, such as roses or carnations

Two red candles and two candle stands

We often forget that food is magical, particularly in its ability to sustain our body in health and well-being. Food is also highly susceptible to absorbing the grower's or cook's emotions.

A great number of foodstuffs magically correspond to love, such as chocolate, hazelnuts, mangoes, cinnamon, cloves, cherries, pistachios, rose flavoring, strawberries and vanilla. Most of this type of food is sweet-tasting, or fleshy in texture, such as avocados.

Food prepared with love and care will enhance the feeling of nurture and harmony in any social gathering. Kitchen magic is basically being aware of the energy within food and directing that energy toward a particular purpose.

This is a very simple spell, which requires you to add not only certain spices and foods to a meal that you prepare specially to honor your loved one, but also a feeling of nurturing and care.

What should I do?

Light the rose-colored candle in the kitchen or near a spot where you will do most of your preparation for the meal.

As you prepare the meal, chop, wash and mix the ingredients with your focus on giving love and nurturing your loved one. Imagine him or her eating the food and feeling happy and well-cared for. Use the finest ingredients you can afford and, if possible, cook only with steel, copper or iron cooking utensils.

When using heat, imagine the fire imparting warmth not only to the food, but also to the heart of your loved one.

Set the table, again with care and consideration, and place the flowers in a low bowl in the center of the table with the red candles on either side.

When you are ready to eat, light the candles and say a little prayer of thankfulness and protection for your love.

When should I do this spell?

During the phase of a full moon

Honoring Your Friendship: Making a Friendship Bag to Share

What do I need?

Natural fabric that is rose-colored or a shade of red or purple

Your favorite threads, beads, ribbons and buttons

A white candle

A small present for each bag other than your own

A friendship bag creates a continuing bond between you and your friend or group of friends, and allows you to honor one another's friendship.

You and a friend can make a small bag to give to each other. If a larger group of friends wants to participate, each person could nominate making some part of the bags. For example, if three friends are involved, one can sew the edges of all three bags, another can do some embroidery for the three bags, while yet another sews on the decorative beads as a finishing touch.

By combining your energies together in a creative project you have worked a powerful form of magic to enhance your friendship.

What should I do?

Use your fabric and decorations to make rich, lush-looking bags. They can be any size – one convenient and favorable size is 6 ⅜–8 inches (16.8–20.8 cm) wide and 8–10 ⅝ inches (20.8–27.5 cm) long.

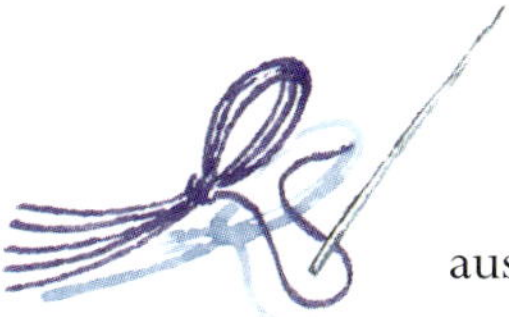

Feng shui practitioners believe that different sizes resonate with auspicious or inauspicious energies. The measurement between $6\frac{3}{8}$–8 inches resonates with helpful people, while 8–$10\frac{5}{8}$ inches corresponds to honor and reward.

When you have finished the bags, gather together at the time of a full moon and light a white candle. Place the bags on either side of the candle, or around the candle at a safe distance from falling wax. Hold hands and chant the following words:

"Nurture [name], love [name], honor [name]."

Repeat this chant again and again, varying it for each cycle by inserting the name of a different person in the circle. Continue chanting, inserting names at random until you feel a strong force of energy weaving around you, connecting you to one another.

When ready, each person places a small present in each bag, signifying the love you have for one another. The present could be a crystal that you feel resonates with your friend's energy, a stone from a shared favorite place, a poem, a special rune, or any other object that you feel moved to give your friend or friends that will not take up too much room in the bag.

When should I do this spell?

During one full cycle of the moon (over 28 days)

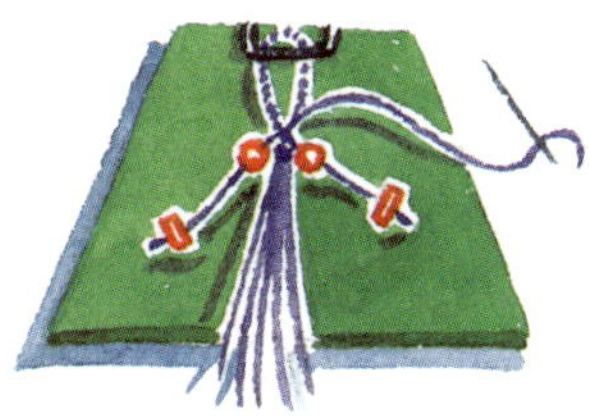

Spells When Things Go Wrong

Avoiding Unwanted Attentions

What do I need?

Visualization skills

When faced with demands by an unwanted suitor or a stranger making unwelcome advances, focus on your inner strength and realize that you have the power to say "No."

In these situations, it pays to use your common sense, and not lose your sense of goodwill by lashing out and being unkind or mean. The latter solution only indicates that you are feeling fearful and are not in control of the situation. Remember, any unkindness tends to rebound threefold back to the person who shows it.

Try the following spell to give you an extra edge when dealing with intrusive people.

What should I do?

When faced with unwanted attention, immediately ground yourself. This means that you must become conscious of the energy of the ground under your feet. Imagine that a blue line of energy is moving from the ground, through your feet and up through your body to your head.

Imagine this blue line expanding until it entirely encloses you within its glow. Keep this image in your head all the time you are talking to your unwanted suitor or being watched by an unsavory character.

Feel the blue, safe cocoon you have created around yourself as a cloak with a deep hood, which completely covers you and allows you to move quickly and silently.

Watch the reactions of the other person. When their eyes start sliding away from you, as if they are having trouble focusing on you, that is when you need to politely leave the situation.

When you are away from the situation, ground the blue light by imagining it compressing into a blue line that travels back down into the earth. Don't forget to do this – if you don't, you will soon wonder why your friends are not talking to you.

When should I do this spell?

Any time you feel threatened or uncomfortable

Healing Rifts and Quarrels

What do I need?

A smudge stick made from good quality sage

A box of matches

Two heavy sticks (or clapping sticks)

A copper bowl half-filled with sand

When arguments occur on a regular basis, it may be an indication that there are a number of deep-seated problems in the relationship. Sometimes these arguments have nothing to do with the real problem – they are like a smokescreen that hides the real issues.

The atmosphere that is created tends to accumulate over time and can, in itself, predispose you and your partner to fighting. This accumulation of an atmosphere of anger and frustration must be cleared before a real healing of the relationship can begin.

What should I do?

Early in the morning of the start of a new phase of the moon, light a smudge stick and carry it around the house in a counter-clockwise direction. You may either walk around the outside of the house or walk along the walls of the interior with your smudge stick.

Place the smudge stick in the copper bowl half-filled with sand and let it smolder in the center of the house. Now, pick up your two heavy sticks.

Identify where most of your arguments occur in the house. Once you have isolated these areas, walk to the nearest corner of each spot and loudly hit your sticks together. Imagine that you are scaring the arguments out of the house, thus giving yourselves a chance to communicate properly.

When you have used the sticks in a corner of all of your "argument areas," take your smudge stick and make sweeping motions, visualizing that you are moving and cleansing the bad energy out of the house and out of your lives.

When should I do this spell?

During the phase of a new moon

Healing Feelings of Jealousy or Envy

What do I need?

A metal bowl half-filled with sand

A black pen

A piece of paper

A box of matches

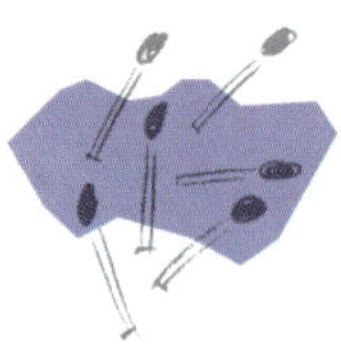

Feeling jealous is related to a feeling that you are powerless to get what you want from life. It is important to understand that we all have our unique path through life and that it is absolutely impossible to compare life situations or try to compete with another person. If this all makes sense but you still feel plagued by feelings of jealousy, try the following spell.

What should I do?

Place your metal bowl containing sand on a stable, fireproof surface. Take your pen and paper and write down the names of all the people of whom you feel jealous. Write the reason you feel jealous of that person beside each name.

If an overwhelming feeling arises concerning a particular person, just write down that person's name, along with all the reasons you feel jealous of them. The sheer act of writing down names and reasons will disperse some of the feelings of jealousy or envy.

If you have several names written down, tear the sheet into segments so that only one name and reason appears on each torn piece of paper.

Fold one of the pieces of paper in half and place it on the sand in your metal bowl. Light a match and burn the paper. Watch the flames consume it and see the smoke rise up.

Imagine that your feelings of jealousy toward that particular person are rising up with the smoke, moving away from you. Repeat this with all the other pieces of paper. When you have finished, dispose of the sand and ashes back into the earth.

When should I do this spell?

During the phase of a full moon or whenever feelings of jealousy overwhelm you

Dealing With Being Hurt

What do I need?

A small stone that you have found on the ground or a small piece of green obsidian

It is inevitable that we will suffer emotional hurt at one time or another. It is important to give yourself time to feel sad about the hurtful action of a person who has been close to you. This spell focuses on using a special stone to help absorb the hurt from your body. If you can find it, use green obsidian. This crystal has the power to help you deal with negative emotions.

What should I do?

Sit in a comfortable chair and hold the green obsidian in your hand. Briefly focus on the hurt you have received and imagine it in terms of physical pain. Where does it hurt in your body? Can you feel it in your chest, your stomach, your throat?

Focus now on the feeling of physical discomfort in your body. Place the stone or crystal on the area, and imagine that the stone is absorbing the hurt, and that the area is becoming less and less sore and tender.

When you feel that the stone or crystal has absorbed all the pain, take three deep breaths.

If you used a stone that isn't obsidian, take it to a lake, river, sea or other large body of water near you and throw it as far away from you as possible.

If you used green obsidian, which has great power to deal with negativity, wash it under running water, then soak it in salted water for three days and nights. Keep it for when you need to use it again.

When should I do this spell?

Any time you feel hurt and rejected

Dealing With Possessive Relationships

This spell focuses on helping you seal yourself from invasive, possessive relationships. This spell involves combining the four elements – earth, air, fire and water – to make a potion that can help protect you from obsessive, intrusive behavior.

What do I need?

A table

An incense stick, preferably frankincense

A small white candle

A box of matches

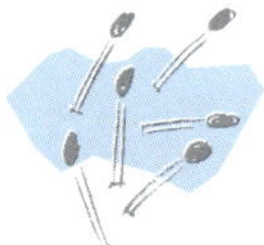

A rosebud on a short stem with any thorns shaved off

A small jar of water

A small bowl or box of salt

What should I do?

Collect your ingredients and arrange them on a small table in a place where you will not be disturbed. Imagine that a line of blue light is glowing in a circle around you. Visualize this glow extending up from the floor and curving over your head, creating a tent to help protect you from disturbances.

Light the incense and the candle. Take the rosebud and pass it over the smoking incense, saying the following words:

"Let the powers of air give me strength and protection."

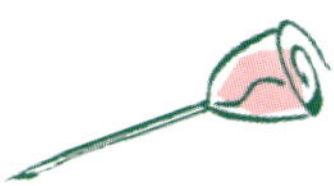

Pass the rosebud over the flame of the candle, saying the following words:

"Let the powers of fire give me strength and protection."

Dip the rosebud into the jar of water, saying the following words:

"Let the powers of water give me strength and protection."

Dip the rosebud into the bowl of salt, saying the following words:

"Let the powers of earth give me strength and protection."

Now pour the salt into the jar of water. Lift the jar and pass it over the top of the incense and candle flame. Dip the rosebud into the salty water and glide the flower over your eyelids, your ears, your nostrils, your mouth, your nipples, your navel and the openings between your legs. This will help protect you from invasive behavior.

When should I do this spell?

During the phase of a full moon

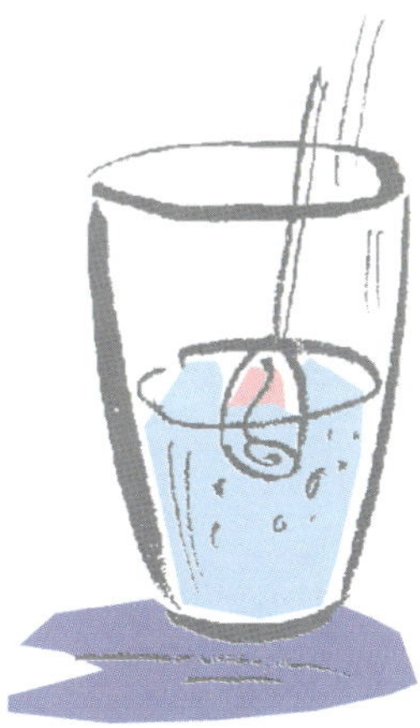

Helping You Say Goodbye

What do I need?

A picture of the person who has passed away

A sprig of rosemary

An object that the deceased had given you out of love

A white candle and a stable candle holder

A fragrance that reminds you of your friend, relative or partner, or lavender essential oil

There are unhappy times when we have to say goodbye to a friend, relative or partner who has passed away. The pain of this loss is almost unbearable at first. No spell can deaden the feeling of loss. However, try the following spell to help you say goodbye with honor and dignity.

What should I do?

Assemble your ingredients and tools on a shelf or other spot where the arrangement won't be disturbed. Set up the picture of the person, and place the rosemary in front of the picture, along with their personal gift to you.

Wipe the candle with the fragrance or lavender oil, place it in the candle holder, and position it behind the picture. When you are ready, light the candle and pick up the gift.

Feel the person's energy in the gift and remember the link between you. Use this feeling to say your goodbyes and to wish him or her safe passage. Take this opportunity to feel the loved one's soothing presence with you and feel them comforting you.

When you feel ready, extinguish the candle. Use this spell whenever you feel the need to be comforted.

When should I do this spell?

Within three weeks of your loved one's time of passing

Coping With Loss

What do I need?

Your favorite drink

A wineglass, chalice or goblet

A single tear

This spell focuses on the correspondence between emotions and the element of water.

What should I do?

Pour your favorite drink into the glass or cup, then mix a single tear with the liquid. Go outside or stand near a window in full view of the moon. Raise the glass or cup and feel the energy of the moon captured in the liquid held above your head.

Imagine the energy of the moon moving down your arms, body and feet. Visualize this energy connecting with the flow of the earth's energy.

Drink the enchanted potion, leaving a small mouthful. Pour the remaining liquid into the ground, imagining that your sadness is flowing away with it, into the earth.

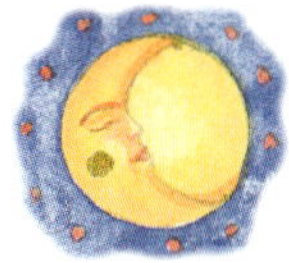

When should I do this spell?

Whenever you feel sad, preferably when the moon is waning (growing smaller)

Coping With Hatred

What do I need?

A cup of sea salt

A bowl of water

A bunch of fennel

Black silk ribbons

Drawing pins

A symbol of the pentacle for protection (optional)

This spell is designed to help you seal your home against intense negative energies, using the strong psychic cleansing properties of sea salt and the protective qualities of fennel.

What should I do?

First, count the number of windows and external doors in your home. Pour the salt into the bowl of water and divide the bunch of fennel into small bundles – one bundle for each window and external door. Tie each bundle with a black silk ribbon.

Take the bowl and lightly sprinkle the salted water around the edges of all your windows and external doors. When finished, take the fennel and hang one bundle over each opening to your house. This will help protect you and your home from hatred and other intense emotional imbalances.

For everyday protection, wear the symbol of the pentacle or another talisman that has protective qualities for you.

When should I do this spell?

During the phase of a full moon

Spells to Answer Your Innermost Questions

What do I need?

Four drops of rose geranium essential oil

An oil burner filled with water and a tea light

A box of matches

One apple

A sharp paring knife

A metal bowl to catch the apple peel

What is the Name of My True Love?

A great many traditional spells exist for finding out the name of your true love. After casting this spell, you may be surprised by the name that comes through. Maybe it is someone you know already.

Once you have worked out the name of your true love, you can use a pendulum or even flip a coin to ask whether you already have met your true love. For instructions on how to use a pendulum, see pages 72–73.

What should I do?

Measure out the essential oil, light the oil burner and sit in a comfortable chair with the bowl at your feet and the knife and the apple beside you. Place the oil burner near you so that you can smell the scent and see the tea light burning.

Concentrate on the smell of rose geranium and start consciously breathing in for a count of four and out for a count of four. Feel that you are letting go of all your everyday concerns. Focus your mind on finding out the name of your true love.

When you feel focused and calm, pick up the apple and the paring knife and say:

"With this knife I shall carve out the first letter of my true love's name."

Peel the apple with your right hand if you are right-handed, or with your left hand if you are left-handed. Try to keep the line of the peel unbroken as long as possible. When the peel breaks, allow it to land in the bowl. See if the shape in which the peel has fallen forms a letter.

Even if you cannot discern a letter, concentrate on the shape of the peel. The first name that pops into your head will be the name of your true love.

When should I do this spell?

On a Friday evening

What Will My True Love be Like?

What do I need?

A piece of parchment or parchment-like paper

Your favorite pen

A length of red ribbon

Red fabric made of natural fibers

A journal

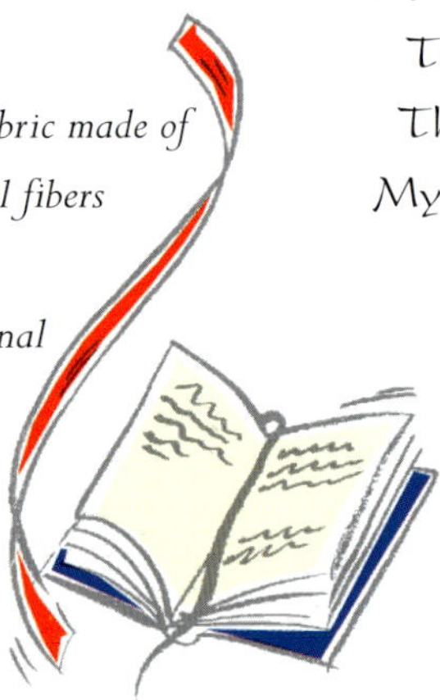

This spell focuses on accessing your dreams to give you a picture of what your true love is like. Speaking the charm before you go to sleep will encourage your subconscious to give you a clue about your true love's qualities, and perhaps a hint as to his or her identity.

What should I do?

On the sheet of parchment or paper, write the following charm:

The face, the form, the touch, the voice;
The love to make my heart rejoice.
The name and nature unconcealed;
My love, in dreams, shall be revealed.

– Liam Cyfrin

When you have memorized the charm, roll the paper up tightly and tie it with the red ribbon. Wrap it in red cloth, then put it under your pillow. Place your journal and pen on your bedside table, so that when you wake up you can write down the immediate impressions of your dreams. These dreams will give you the clues you need to tell you what your true love will be like.

When should I do this spell?

On a Friday evening, just before you go to sleep

Is He or She the Right Person for Me?

What do I need?

An article of clothing or a lock of hair from your lover

A crystal pendulum hanging from a chain

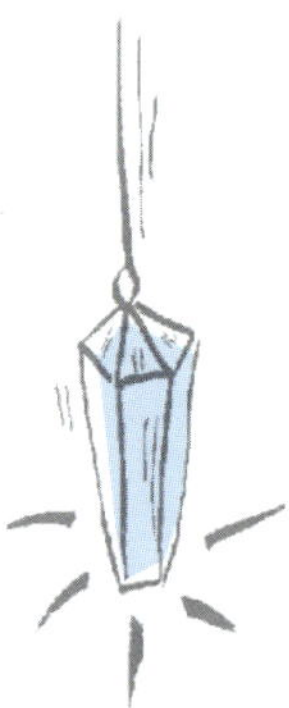

This spell focuses on using a pendulum. A pendulum is a useful tool that taps into a form of universal intelligence. It can indicate the answer to questions, such as whether or not your lover is the right person for you. This is a useful spell if you are confused by conflicting advice and feelings, because it helps you use your instincts when making your decision.

What should I do?

If you are not familiar with using pendulums, take some time to get the feel of it. The pendulum chain should be held between your thumb and forefinger. If you are right-handed, hold it in your right hand. If you are left-handed, hold it in your left hand.

The pendulum answers questions with a "yes" or a "no" answer. To work out what its movements mean, try some test questions. For example, ask:

"Is my name [insert your real name]?"

Observe which way the pendulum swings. This will be the direction of the "yes" swing. Do a similar exercise to identify the "no" swing.

When you feel ready, place the item from your lover on a table near your elbow so that you can comfortably hang the pendulum from its chain directly over the item. Focus on your breathing and let go of all everyday concerns, concentrating only on the question that you wish to ask. When you've reached a deep, meditative state, ask the following question as the pendulum hangs over your lover's item:

"Is [insert name of lover] the right person for me at this moment in time?"

The pendulum will give you an answer. You may wish to ask it other questions concerning your relationship to give you further insight into what is or is not right for you.

When should I do this spell?

On a Friday evening

Does He or She Love Me?

What do I need?

A clear quartz crystal

An unpolished rose quartz crystal

A rose quartz crystal that is polished but irregularly shaped

A rose quartz crystal in the shape of a heart

A smoky quartz crystal

A bag or velvet-lined box in which to store your stones

Try the following spell when you are in the very early stages of courtship and you and your partner are not too certain of each other. It can also be useful in long-term relationships in which one person may feel taken for granted.

What should I do?

Three days before doing this spell (Tuesday evening), wash the stones in salty water, then in clear running water. Let the stones dry naturally, then put them into the bag or box.

On the Friday night, sit comfortably and concentrate on your breathing. Clear your mind and focus on whether the person you are asking about loves you. Hold the clear quartz crystal in your hand and repeat the person's name 24 times. Place the crystal on the ground in front of you.

Take the other stones from the box and hold all of them in your hands while you ask your question. Throw the stones onto the ground and see which stone is nearest to the clear quartz crystal.

If the stone closest to the clear quartz is the one that is unpolished, this indicates that the person loves you but doesn't know it yet. If the stone is polished into a smooth, pebble shape, the person loves you but is not ready to express their emotion.

If the stone closest to the clear quartz is the one shaped into a heart, this indicates that the person loves you and is ready to connect with you. If the stone is the smoky quartz, this means that the person does not love you. . . yet.

When should I do this spell?

On a Friday evening

Will This Relationship Last?

What do I need?

An oil burner filled with water

A tea light and some matches

Four drops of cinnamon essential oil

The Lovers card, a major arcana card, from your favorite Tarot deck

Your journal

Your favorite pen

One of the important aspects of magic is that, by casting spells, you are accepting responsibility for the direction in which you want your life to go. Which way a relationship will grow is truly within your own control. The spell below will help you tap into your instincts to help guide you toward enjoying the relationship you have or finding one that will suit you better.

What should I do?

Gather your tools and ingredients and find a safe and comfortable place in which you will not be disturbed. Set up the oil burner and tea light, and measure out the essential oil. Light the candle and breathe in the scent of cinnamon.

Focus on your breathing and feel yourself letting go of your daily worries. Look at the image on the Lovers card. Examine it in great detail. Feel as if you are falling into the image.

In this relaxed state of mind, ask the following question:

"What do I need to do to make this relationship last for the benefit of both myself and [insert name]?"

Continue looking at the card and listen to or watch, in a detached manner, any messages, advice or images that come to your mind. Write these down in your journal. Do not analyze them – just keep writing anything that comes to your mind. Keep going until you feel ready to stop, then immediately close your journal.

Take three deep breaths and turn the Tarot card face down. Open your journal and start to sift through the information. You may be surprised by the information you have been given. Above all, honor what your intuition has told you.

When should I do this spell?

On a Friday evening

Glossary

Amulet – a protective device worn around the neck or hung from the door or window of a sacred space or home.

Chakra – one of the seven major psychic energy centers running through the middle of the body, approximately along the spine. These chakra centers start at the base of the spine and end at the top of the head.

Chalice – or cup, one of the elemental tools symbolizing water and the emotions.

Charm – a magical word or words that can be used in a spell.

Circle – a sacred space, usually thought of as a sphere of energy created when the circle is cast.

Grounding – connecting the body's energy with that of the earth.

Pendulum – a stone or metal weight that is tied to the end of a piece of string or a length of chain. You can make one easily for yourself. Use a smallish, tear-shaped stone (such as an amethyst, quartz crystal or a faceted piece of lead crystal) that has a point at the bottom and a hole drilled at the top, through which you connect a length of chain or string.

Pentacle – a five-pointed star that symbolizes the four elements and the spirit. A metal version of this symbol can be worn as a protection. Make sure that you wear the pentacle with the point uppermost, because this indicates that you are working with constructive energies rather than destructive ones.

Tarot – a deck of cards used as a form of divination. The deck comprises 78 cards, which are divided into the major arcana of 22 cards and the minor arcana of 56 cards. The minor arcana are further divided into four groups, representing the four elements.

Talisman – an object charged to attract a specific magical energy.

Published by Lansdowne Publishing Pty Ltd
Level 1, 18 Argyle Street, Sydney NSW 2000, Australia

First published 2001

Commissioned by Deborah Nixon
Text: Antonia Beattie
Illustrators: Sue Rawkins, Sue Ninham, Joanna Davies, Penny Lovelock
Cover illustration: Sue Ninham
Designer: Sue Rawkins
Editor: Sarah Shrubb
Production Manager: Sally Stokes
Project Co-ordinator: Kylie Lowson

Set in Perpetua, Present and Gigi on QuarkXPress
Printed in China, produced by Jade Productions

National Library of Australia Cataloguing-in-Publication Data

Beattie, Antonia.
Spells for love.

ISBN 1 86302 737 8.

1. Magic 2. Charms 3. Incantations 4. Love. I. Title.

133.44